# Mastering Business Con
# Techniques for Effective Collaboration

Allen Hill

**Copyright © [2023]**

**Title:Mastering Business Communication: Techniques for Effective Collaboration**
**Author's: Allen Hill**

This book was printed and published by [Publisher's: **Allen Hill**] in [2023]

**ISBN:**

# TABLE OF CONTENT

# Chapter 3: Effective Collaboration in the Workplace 25

The Power of Collaboration

Building a Collaborative Work Environment

Effective Team Communication

Resolving Conflicts and Disagreements

# Chapter 4: Tools and Technologies for Business Communication 34

Email and Instant Messaging Etiquette

Video Conferencing and Virtual Meetings

Project Management and Collaboration Software

Social Media for Professional Communication

## Chapter 8: Effective Communication in Leadership Roles 66

## Chapter 9: Communication in Remote and Virtual Work Environments 74

## Chapter 10: Effective Negotiation and Conflict Resolution 82

# Chapter 1: The Importance of Effective Business Communication

## Understanding the Role of Communication in Business

Effective communication is an essential skill in today's fast-paced business environment. Whether you work in a small startup or a multinational corporation, the ability to convey ideas, share information, and collaborate with colleagues is crucial for success. In this subchapter, we will explore the importance of communication in the business environment and provide techniques for employees to improve their communication skills.

Communication plays a pivotal role in every aspect of business. It is the foundation for building relationships, fostering teamwork, and ensuring that everyone is on the same page. In fact, studies have shown that organizations with strong communication practices are more likely to be successful and have higher employee engagement.

One of the key benefits of effective communication is its ability to enhance productivity. When employees can clearly understand their roles, responsibilities, and objectives, they are more likely to perform at their best. Communication also facilitates the sharing of information, making it easier for employees to access the resources and knowledge they need to excel in their work.

Furthermore, communication is vital for collaboration in today's interconnected business world. As businesses become increasingly global and teams are spread across different locations, effective communication becomes even more critical. By utilizing various communication channels, such as email, video conferencing, and instant messaging, employees can collaborate seamlessly, regardless of their physical location.

Moreover, communication is not just about conveying information; it also plays a significant role in building strong relationships. When employees communicate effectively with their colleagues, superiors, and clients, trust is established, and stronger working relationships are formed. This, in turn, leads to increased job satisfaction, higher morale, and a more positive work environment.

To improve communication skills in the business environment, employees can implement various techniques. Active listening, for example, is an essential aspect of effective communication. By giving full attention to the speaker, maintaining eye contact, and asking clarifying questions, employees can ensure that they understand the message accurately.

Additionally, employees should practice clear and concise communication. Using simple language, organizing thoughts coherently, and avoiding jargon or technical terms can ensure that the message is easily understood by all stakeholders.

In conclusion, understanding the role of communication in the business environment is crucial for employees seeking to excel in their careers. Effective communication enhances productivity, facilitates collaboration, and builds strong relationships. By implementing techniques such as active listening and clear communication, employees can improve their communication skills and contribute to the success of their organizations.

## Benefits of Effective Communication in the Workplace

In today's fast-paced business environment, effective communication plays a crucial role in the success of any organization. Whether you are an employee or a manager, mastering the art of communication is essential for effective collaboration and achieving desired outcomes. This subchapter will delve into the numerous benefits of effective communication in the workplace and shed light on how it can positively impact the business environment.

One of the primary benefits of effective communication is increased productivity. When employees are able to communicate their thoughts, ideas, and concerns clearly, it eliminates ambiguity and reduces the likelihood of misunderstandings. This clarity leads to better coordination and collaboration among team members, resulting in enhanced productivity and efficiency. Additionally, effective communication enables employees to receive timely feedback and instructions, allowing them to make informed decisions and complete tasks more effectively.

Another advantage of effective communication in the workplace is improved employee morale and engagement. When employees feel that their voices are heard and their opinions matter, they become more engaged and motivated. Effective communication fosters a positive work environment where employees feel comfortable sharing their thoughts and ideas, leading to increased job satisfaction and employee retention.

Furthermore, effective communication helps build strong relationships among team members and promotes a sense of camaraderie. When employees communicate openly and respectfully, it builds trust and fosters a sense of belonging. This, in turn, leads to better teamwork, increased collaboration, and a supportive work environment where everyone feels valued and appreciated.

Effective communication is also crucial for effective problem-solving and conflict resolution. When employees can express their concerns and issues without fear of judgment or reprisal, it facilitates open dialogue and enables the identification of solutions. Moreover, effective communication helps prevent conflicts from escalating and allows for quick resolution, minimizing disruptions in the workplace.

Lastly, effective communication in the workplace enhances the overall organizational culture. When communication flows smoothly, it promotes transparency, encourages innovation, and creates a shared vision. This results in a positive business environment that attracts and retains top talent, fosters creativity, and drives business success.

In conclusion, mastering effective communication in the workplace is vital in today's business environment. The benefits of effective communication include increased productivity, improved employee morale and engagement, stronger relationships, efficient problem-solving, and a positive organizational culture. By honing their communication skills, employees can contribute to a more collaborative, productive, and successful business environment.

## Common Barriers to Effective Communication

In today's fast-paced business environment, effective communication plays a pivotal role in ensuring smooth collaboration and achieving organizational goals. However, there are several common barriers that can hinder effective communication within the workplace. By understanding these barriers, employees can proactively address them and enhance their communication skills to foster better collaboration and productivity.

One of the most prevalent barriers to effective communication is a lack of clarity. Misinterpretation of information can occur when messages are not clear, concise, or specific. This can lead to confusion, misunderstandings, and mistakes. To overcome this barrier, employees should strive to communicate with precision, using clear and straightforward language, and ensuring that their messages are easily understood by others.

Another barrier is the presence of noise or distractions in the business environment. Noise can be both physical, such as loud conversations or equipment noise, and psychological, such as personal stress or preoccupation. These distractions can make it difficult for employees to concentrate on the message being delivered, resulting in miscommunication or incomplete understanding. Employees should identify and minimize sources of noise to create a more conducive environment for effective communication.

Lack of feedback is also a significant barrier to effective communication. When there is no opportunity for immediate feedback or clarification, misunderstandings can persist, and issues may go unresolved. Employees should actively seek feedback from their colleagues, superiors, or subordinates to ensure that their messages are being received and understood as intended. This feedback loop helps in identifying and rectifying any communication gaps or misconceptions.

Cultural and language differences can also impede effective communication in a diverse business environment. Different cultures have varying communication styles, norms, and expectations, which can lead to misunderstandings or even offense. Employees should be mindful of cultural differences and adapt their communication style accordingly. Additionally, language barriers can hinder effective communication. In such cases, employees can use translation tools, seek assistance from bilingual colleagues, or invest in language training to bridge the gap.

In conclusion, there are several common barriers to effective communication in the business environment. By recognizing and addressing these barriers, employees can enhance their communication skills, foster better collaboration, and drive organizational success. Clear and concise communication, minimizing distractions, seeking feedback, and being mindful of cultural and language differences are key strategies for overcoming these barriers. The ability to communicate effectively is a valuable skill in the modern workplace and can significantly contribute to professional growth and success.

## Overcoming Communication Challenges

In today's fast-paced business environment, effective communication is paramount to achieving success. However, the reality is that communication challenges are inevitable and can hinder collaboration and productivity in the workplace. This subchapter aims to provide employees with essential techniques for overcoming these obstacles and mastering business communication.

One common challenge in the business environment is the use of different communication styles and preferences among colleagues. To overcome this, it is crucial to foster a culture of understanding and respect. Employees should be encouraged to adapt their communication style to match the preferences of their colleagues, whether it be through written communication, face-to-face meetings, or virtual platforms. By being flexible and open-minded, individuals can bridge the communication gap and enhance collaboration.

Another challenge arises from cultural and language barriers within a diverse workforce. In such cases, it is essential to practice active listening and empathy. Employees should make an effort to understand cultural nuances, use clear and concise language, and avoid jargon or ambiguous terms that may confuse others. Additionally, utilizing visual aids and non-verbal cues can help convey messages more effectively and promote understanding across different backgrounds.

Technological advancements have revolutionized communication, but they also bring their own set of challenges. Remote work, video conferences, and instant messaging platforms have become commonplace, but they can sometimes hinder effective communication. To overcome these challenges, employees should prioritize clarity and brevity in their communication, be mindful of time zones and availability, and establish guidelines for virtual meetings to ensure everyone is engaged and heard.

Misunderstandings and conflicts can also arise due to poor communication. To address this challenge, employees should practice active communication by seeking clarification, repeating information, and summarizing discussions. Additionally, regular feedback and constructive criticism can help identify and rectify any communication gaps or errors, fostering continuous improvement in the workplace.

Ultimately, overcoming communication challenges requires a collective effort from all employees. By embracing adaptability, empathy, and effective listening skills, individuals can enhance collaboration, build stronger relationships, and contribute to a more harmonious and productive business environment.

In conclusion, mastering business communication is crucial for success in today's dynamic workplace. This subchapter has outlined various techniques to overcome communication challenges, including adapting to different communication styles, bridging cultural and language barriers, navigating technological advancements, and resolving misunderstandings. By implementing these strategies, employees can significantly enhance their communication skills and contribute to a more collaborative and efficient business environment.

# Chapter 2: Developing Strong Communication Skills

## Verbal Communication Techniques

In today's rapidly evolving business environment, effective communication is more crucial than ever before. As employees, we must master the art of verbal communication in order to succeed and thrive in our professional lives. This subchapter aims to equip you with essential techniques to enhance your verbal communication skills and excel in the business environment.

1. Active Listening: Effective communication begins with active listening. Engage fully in conversations by maintaining eye contact, nodding to show understanding, and asking relevant questions. Avoid interrupting and truly focus on understanding the speaker's message. By actively listening, you can build stronger relationships, foster collaboration, and demonstrate respect for your colleagues.

2. Clear and Concise Language: In a fast-paced business environment, clarity is key. Use simple and concise language to convey your ideas, ensuring that your message is easily understood by your audience. Avoid jargon, acronyms, and technical terms that may confuse others. Practice being articulate, organized, and to the point in your verbal communication.

3. Non-Verbal Cues: Remember that communication is not just about words; non-verbal cues play a significant role as well. Pay attention to your body language, facial expressions, and gestures. Maintain an open and

approachable posture to encourage conversation and collaboration. Respect personal space and be mindful of cultural differences that may influence non-verbal communication.

4.     Empathy     and     Emotional     Intelligence: Developing empathy and emotional intelligence is vital in the business environment. By understanding and considering the emotions of others, you can tailor your communication to be more empathetic and supportive. This skill fosters stronger relationships, resolves conflicts, and promotes effective teamwork.

5.               Constructive               Feedback: Providing and receiving feedback is an essential aspect of effective communication. Practice giving constructive feedback by focusing on specific behaviors and offering suggestions for improvement. Similarly, be open to receiving feedback without becoming defensive. Embrace feedback as an opportunity for growth and improvement.

6.                         Adaptability: In today's diverse and multicultural workplace, adaptability is crucial. Be mindful of the different communication styles and preferences of your colleagues. Adjust your communication approach to fit the needs of your audience, whether it be face-to-face conversations, phone calls, or virtual meetings. Flexibility in communication is key to building strong relationships and effective collaboration.

By mastering these verbal communication techniques, we can enhance our professional relationships, foster collaboration, and achieve success in the ever-evolving business environment. Remember, effective communication is a skill that can be honed and refined over time. Practice these techniques consistently, and watch your communication skills soar!

## Nonverbal Communication Strategies

In today's fast-paced business environment, effective communication is crucial for success. While verbal communication plays a significant role in conveying information, nonverbal communication can often be even more powerful in influencing others and achieving desired outcomes. Understanding and mastering nonverbal communication strategies is essential for employees in the business environment to enhance their collaborative efforts and achieve their goals.

1. Body Language: Nonverbal cues such as facial expressions, hand gestures, and posture can convey emotions and intentions. Employees should pay attention to their body language, ensuring that it aligns with their verbal communication. Maintaining eye contact, adopting an open posture, and using appropriate hand movements can all contribute to conveying confidence, credibility, and engagement.

2. Facial Expressions: The face is a canvas of emotions. A smile can create a positive and welcoming atmosphere, while frowns or raised eyebrows may indicate confusion or disagreement. Understanding the impact of facial expressions and learning to control them can significantly improve communication in the business environment.

3. Tone and Pitch: The way an employee speaks can convey a wealth of information. It is crucial to consider the tone and pitch of their voice when communicating with others. Speaking with a clear and confident voice can help convey authority and credibility, while a gentle and empathetic tone can help build rapport and trust.

4. Personal Space: Respect for personal space is vital in the business environment. Being aware of appropriate distances when interacting

with colleagues or clients shows professionalism and consideration. Invading personal space can make others uncomfortable, while maintaining a respectful distance fosters a positive and comfortable environment.

5. Active Listening: Nonverbal cues can also be utilized when listening to others. Nodding, maintaining eye contact, and using facial expressions to reflect understanding and engagement can encourage open and effective communication. Active listening demonstrates respect and interest, leading to stronger relationships and improved collaboration.

By mastering these nonverbal communication strategies, employees can enhance their interactions within the business environment. Effective nonverbal communication not only strengthens relationships but also helps individuals convey their ideas, influence others positively, and achieve their goals more effectively. Developing these skills will not only benefit employees in their current roles but also enhance their overall professional growth and success.

## Active Listening Skills

In today's fast-paced business environment, effective communication is crucial for achieving success. One of the most important skills for employees to develop is active listening. Active listening goes beyond simply hearing what someone is saying; it involves fully engaging with the speaker, understanding their message, and providing appropriate responses. Mastering active listening skills can greatly enhance collaboration and productivity in the business environment.

Active listening starts with giving the speaker your undivided attention. In a world filled with distractions, it can be challenging to focus solely on the person speaking. However, making a conscious effort to eliminate distractions and actively engage with the speaker demonstrates respect and shows that you value their input. Maintain eye contact, nod occasionally, and use non-verbal cues to show that you are actively listening.

Another essential aspect of active listening is seeking clarification when needed. Sometimes, the speaker may use unfamiliar jargon or present complex ideas. Rather than pretending to understand, ask questions to ensure you grasp their message accurately. This not only clarifies any confusion but also shows the speaker that you are genuinely interested in understanding their perspective.

Paraphrasing and summarizing are crucial active listening techniques that help ensure effective communication. After the speaker has finished conveying their message, paraphrase or summarize what you understood to confirm your comprehension. This not only ensures that you interpreted their message correctly but also shows that you are actively engaged in the conversation.

Active listening also involves being empathetic and understanding the speaker's emotions and underlying messages. Pay attention to their tone of voice, facial expressions, and body language to gain a deeper understanding of their feelings and intentions. Responding empathetically, such as by acknowledging their emotions or providing support, helps build trust and strengthens relationships in the business environment.

Finally, active listening also includes providing appropriate feedback. Responding thoughtfully and constructively to the speaker's message demonstrates that you have truly absorbed their words. Avoid interrupting and wait for the speaker to finish before offering your input. This shows respect for their ideas and encourages open and honest communication.

In conclusion, active listening is a vital skill for employees in the business environment. By giving undivided attention, seeking clarification, paraphrasing and summarizing, showing empathy, and providing appropriate feedback, employees can enhance collaboration and productivity. Mastering active listening skills not only improves communication but also fosters positive relationships and a more inclusive work environment.

## Written Communication Best Practices

In today's fast-paced business environment, effective written communication has become more important than ever. Emails, memos, reports, and other written documents are the primary means of communication in many organizations. Therefore, it is crucial for employees to master the art of written communication to ensure effective collaboration within the business environment.

1. Clear and Concise Language: When writing for business purposes, it is important to use clear and concise language. Avoid using jargon or technical terms that may confuse the reader. Keep sentences and paragraphs short and to the point, ensuring that your message is easily understood.

2. Organize your Thoughts: Before putting pen to paper or fingers to the keyboard, take a moment to organize your thoughts. Create an outline or a draft to help structure your writing. This will ensure that your message flows logically and coherently, making it easier for the reader to follow.

3. Grammar and Spelling: Poor grammar and spelling mistakes can undermine your credibility and professionalism. Always proofread your writing carefully to eliminate any errors. If grammar and spelling are not your strong suit, consider using grammar-checking software or seeking assistance from a colleague.

4. Tone and Politeness: The tone of your written communication can greatly impact how your message is received. Always strive to maintain a polite and professional tone. Avoid using aggressive or

confrontational language, as it can lead to misunderstandings or strained relationships.

5. Use of Visuals: Visuals such as charts, graphs, and tables can help convey complex information more effectively. When appropriate, include visuals in your written communication to enhance understanding and engagement. However, ensure that the visuals are clear and relevant to the message you are trying to convey.

6. Formatting and Structure: Pay attention to the formatting and structure of your written communication. Use headings, subheadings, and bullet points to break up the text and make it easier to read. Use appropriate fonts and styles, and ensure that your document is well-organized and visually appealing.

7. Proofreading and Editing: Never underestimate the importance of proofreading and editing your written communication. Take the time to review your work, checking for errors, inconsistencies, and areas that could be improved. A well-edited document reflects attention to detail and professionalism.

By following these best practices, employees can enhance their written communication skills and improve collaboration in the business environment. Effective written communication not only ensures clarity and understanding but also helps build strong professional relationships. Remember, practice makes perfect, so make a conscious effort to incorporate these practices into your daily communication routine.

# Chapter 3: Effective Collaboration in the Workplace

## The Power of Collaboration

In today's fast-paced and competitive business environment, the power of collaboration cannot be underestimated. As employees, we often find ourselves working within teams or departments, and it is through effective collaboration that we can achieve remarkable outcomes and drive success for our organizations. This subchapter will delve into the techniques and strategies that will help us master the art of collaboration and enhance our business communication skills.

Collaboration is more than just working together; it is a mindset that fosters open communication, trust, and synergy among team members. When we collaborate effectively, we tap into the collective knowledge, skills, and perspectives of our colleagues, creating a powerful force that propels us towards our goals.

One of the key aspects of effective collaboration is communication. We must learn to actively listen to our team members, share ideas, and provide constructive feedback. By doing so, we create an environment where everyone feels valued and encouraged to contribute their unique insights. Furthermore, clear and concise communication ensures that everyone is on the same page and working towards a common objective.

Another essential element of collaboration is building trust and fostering strong relationships within our teams. Trust is the foundation upon which successful collaborations are built, and it is cultivated through open and honest communication, mutual respect, and accountability. When we trust our colleagues, we are more willing to share ideas, take risks, and support each other's growth.

Collaboration also requires effective leadership. As employees, we can take on leadership roles within our teams by taking initiative, inspiring others, and facilitating the exchange of ideas. A strong leader encourages collaboration by setting clear goals, providing guidance, and empowering team members to make decisions and take ownership of their work.

Lastly, technology has revolutionized collaboration in the business environment. With the advent of various digital tools and platforms, we can now collaborate seamlessly across different locations and time zones. From video conferencing to project management software, these technological advancements enable us to communicate and work together efficiently, irrespective of physical barriers.

In conclusion, the power of collaboration is a game-changer in today's business environment. By mastering the art of collaboration, we can harness the collective intelligence of our teams, foster innovation, and achieve extraordinary results. Effective communication, trust, leadership, and leveraging technology are the pillars that support successful collaborations. As employees, it is essential for us to embrace the power of collaboration and continuously hone our business communication skills to thrive in the competitive world of business.

## Building a Collaborative Work Environment

In today's fast-paced business environment, it is crucial for employees to work together effectively and efficiently to achieve common goals. Collaboration has become a key driver of success, as it fosters innovation, enhances productivity, and creates a positive work culture. This subchapter aims to provide valuable insights and techniques for employees in the business environment to build a collaborative work environment.

1.          Importance          of          Collaboration: Collaboration brings together diverse perspectives, skills, and strengths to solve complex problems and generate creative ideas. It promotes open communication, trust, and mutual respect among team members, leading to increased productivity and job satisfaction.

2.          Effective          Communication: Clear and concise communication is the foundation of collaboration. Employees must actively listen, articulate their ideas, and provide constructive feedback. Utilizing various communication tools, such as emails, video conferencing, and project management software, can facilitate effective collaboration, especially in remote work settings.

3.          Establishing          Trust: Trust is vital for a collaborative work environment. Employees should be encouraged to take risks and share their thoughts openly without fear of judgment or reprisal. Managers can foster trust by recognizing and appreciating individual contributions, promoting transparency, and encouraging teamwork.

4. Team Building Activities: Engaging in team-building activities outside of work can help foster stronger relationships and improve collaboration. Team building exercises, workshops, and social events allow employees to get to know one another on a personal level and build trust, ultimately enhancing collaboration within the workplace.

5. Leveraging Technology: In today's digital era, technology plays a crucial role in facilitating collaboration. Utilizing project management software, cloud-based platforms, and collaborative tools can streamline communication, project tracking, and knowledge sharing, enabling employees to work together seamlessly.

6. Promoting a Positive Work Culture: Creating a positive work culture is essential for fostering collaboration. Encouraging a sense of community, recognizing and celebrating achievements, and providing opportunities for professional growth and development can motivate employees to collaborate effectively.

7. Conflict Resolution: Conflicts are inevitable in any workplace, but addressing them promptly and constructively is vital for maintaining a collaborative work environment. Encouraging open dialogue, active listening, and finding mutually beneficial solutions can help resolve conflicts and strengthen collaboration among team members.

In conclusion, building a collaborative work environment is essential for employees in the business environment to thrive. By emphasizing effective communication, trust-building, team-building activities, leveraging technology, promoting a positive work culture, and resolving conflicts constructively, employees can create an environment that fosters collaboration, innovation, and success.

## Effective Team Communication

In today's fast-paced business environment, effective team communication is vital for the success and productivity of any organization. Clear and efficient communication among team members is the key to achieving common goals and fostering a collaborative work environment. This subchapter will delve into the various techniques and strategies that employees can adopt to enhance their team communication skills.

One of the fundamental aspects of effective team communication is active listening. By actively listening to your teammates, you demonstrate respect and understanding, which promotes trust and open dialogue. To actively listen, maintain eye contact, avoid interrupting, and provide feedback or ask clarifying questions when necessary. This practice not only helps you grasp the message accurately but also ensures that everyone's opinions are valued and considered.

Another essential component of effective team communication is effective verbal communication. Clearly and concisely conveying your ideas, thoughts, and concerns is crucial for avoiding misunderstandings and promoting a cohesive team dynamic. When communicating verbally, use simple and straightforward language, avoid jargon or technical terms, and speak with confidence and clarity. Additionally, be mindful of your tone and body language, as they can significantly impact the effectiveness of your message.

Written communication also plays a pivotal role in team collaboration. Emails, memos, and project reports are common forms of written communication in the business environment. To ensure clarity in written communication, use proper grammar and punctuation, organize your thoughts logically, and proofread your message before sending it. Additionally, be mindful of your audience and tailor your writing style accordingly.

Effective team communication also involves non-verbal cues, such as facial expressions, gestures, and posture. Being aware of these non-verbal cues can help you gauge your teammates' reactions, emotions, and level of engagement during meetings or discussions. Paying attention to these cues allows you to adjust your communication style to ensure optimal understanding and collaboration.

Lastly, embracing technology can significantly enhance team communication in today's digital age. Utilize communication tools such as instant messaging, video conferencing, and project management software to facilitate real-time collaboration, regardless of physical location. However, it is crucial to strike a balance between virtual communication and face-to-face interactions to maintain a personal connection within the team.

In conclusion, effective team communication is a critical skill in the dynamic business environment. By actively listening, practicing effective verbal and written communication, being mindful of non-verbal cues, and leveraging technology, employees can foster a collaborative and productive team culture. These techniques will not only enhance individual performance but also contribute to the overall success of the organization.

## Resolving Conflicts and Disagreements

In the fast-paced and competitive world of the business environment, conflicts and disagreements are bound to arise. Whether it's a difference in opinions, conflicting goals, or a misunderstanding, these situations can hinder effective collaboration and productivity within a team. However, if handled correctly, conflicts can also provide opportunities for growth and innovation. In this subchapter, we will explore techniques for resolving conflicts and disagreements in the business environment.

The first step towards resolving conflicts is to acknowledge their existence. As employees, it is crucial to recognize when conflicts arise and address them promptly. Ignoring conflicts will only allow them to escalate and potentially damage working relationships. By acknowledging conflicts, employees can take proactive steps to seek resolution and prevent further complications.

Once conflicts are acknowledged, effective communication becomes paramount. To resolve conflicts, employees should engage in open and honest discussions with the individuals involved. Active listening is crucial during these discussions, as it shows respect and validates the concerns of all parties. Encouraging each person to express their viewpoint without interruption can lead to a more comprehensive understanding of the issues at hand.

Another technique for resolving conflicts is finding common ground. Encourage employees to identify shared goals or interests to foster a sense of collaboration and cooperation. By focusing on common objectives, individuals can work together towards finding mutually beneficial solutions. This approach helps shift the perspective from an individualistic mindset to a more collective mindset, promoting teamwork and unity.

In some cases, conflicts may require the intervention of a mediator or manager. If an issue seems to be escalating or if the parties involved are unable to find a resolution on their own, seeking assistance from a neutral third party can be beneficial. Mediators can provide a fresh perspective and help facilitate a constructive dialogue between conflicting parties, leading to a more objective and fair resolution.

Finally, it is essential to learn from conflicts and disagreements. By reflecting on the experience, employees can gain insights into their own communication styles and identify areas for improvement. Encourage individuals to approach conflicts as learning opportunities and to develop strategies for preventing similar situations in the future.

In conclusion, conflicts and disagreements are unavoidable in the business environment. However, by acknowledging their existence, engaging in effective communication, finding common ground, seeking assistance when needed, and learning from the experience, employees can successfully resolve conflicts and transform them into opportunities for growth and enhanced collaboration. By mastering the techniques outlined in this subchapter, employees can contribute to a more harmonious and productive business environment.

# Chapter 4: Tools and Technologies for Business Communication

## Email and Instant Messaging Etiquette

In today's fast-paced and interconnected business environment, effective communication is crucial for successful collaboration among employees. Email and instant messaging have become integral tools for exchanging information, ideas, and updates. However, to maintain professionalism and avoid misunderstandings, it is essential to follow proper etiquette when using these communication channels.

1. Think Before You Send: Before hitting the send button, carefully consider the content and tone of your message. Remember, electronic communications are permanent records, and once sent, they cannot be retracted. Always ensure that your message is concise, clear, and free from grammatical errors. Avoid using excessive capitalization, slang, or jargon that might confuse the recipient.

2. Use Appropriate Subject Lines: Subject lines provide a glimpse into the content of your email or instant message. Make sure to use a subject that accurately reflects the purpose of your communication. This allows recipients to prioritize and efficiently manage their inbox. Avoid using generic or vague subjects that may lead to your message being overlooked or ignored.

3. Respect Others' Time: In a busy business environment, time is a valuable resource. Keep your emails and instant messages concise and to the point. Be mindful of the recipient's workload and avoid bombarding them with unnecessary information. If the conversation

becomes lengthy or complex, consider scheduling a face-to-face meeting or a phone call to ensure effective communication.

4. Be Mindful of Tone: Without facial expressions and body language, it is easy for messages to be misinterpreted. Use a polite and professional tone, even when discussing challenging or contentious topics. Avoid using sarcasm, jokes, or overly casual language that may be misunderstood or offend the recipient. Take the time to re-read your message before sending it to ensure it conveys the intended tone.

5. Respond Promptly: In a fast-paced business environment, timely responses are crucial. Acknowledge receipt of emails and instant messages promptly, even if you cannot provide a detailed response immediately. If a response requires additional time, inform the sender about when they can expect to hear back from you. By doing so, you demonstrate professionalism and respect for others' time.

6. Use Proper Formatting: Proper formatting can enhance the readability of your emails and instant messages. Use paragraphs, bullet points, and headings to organize information effectively. Avoid using excessive font styles, colors, or emoticons that may distract or confuse the recipient.

By following these email and instant messaging etiquette guidelines, employees can foster effective communication and collaboration in the dynamic business environment. Remember, clear and professional communication helps build strong working relationships, promotes productivity, and enhances overall success in today's fast-paced world.

## Video Conferencing and Virtual Meetings

In today's fast-paced business environment, staying connected and effectively collaborating with colleagues, clients, and partners is crucial for success. With the advancements in technology, video conferencing and virtual meetings have emerged as powerful tools for businesses to communicate and collaborate remotely. This subchapter will delve into the benefits, tips, and best practices for mastering video conferencing and virtual meetings.

One of the significant advantages of video conferencing and virtual meetings is the ability to bridge the geographical gap. Employees can connect with their counterparts in different offices, branches, or even countries, without having to travel. This not only saves time and money but also promotes efficiency and productivity. Furthermore, video conferencing allows for face-to-face communication, fostering a sense of connection and building stronger relationships.

To ensure successful virtual meetings, it is essential to follow certain guidelines. First and foremost, it is crucial to have a well-equipped and reliable video conferencing system. Investing in high-quality equipment and a stable internet connection is vital to avoid technical glitches and disruptions during meetings. Moreover, participants should be well-prepared and familiarize themselves with the video conferencing platform beforehand.

Another critical aspect of virtual meetings is maintaining professionalism. Dress appropriately, just as you would in a face-to-face meeting, and ensure a quiet and professional environment. Background noise can be distracting and hinder effective communication. Additionally, it is crucial to be punctual and respectful of everyone's time. Start the meeting on time, allocate time for each agenda item, and encourage active participation from all attendees.

Engagement and active participation are key to successful virtual meetings. Encourage attendees to turn on their video cameras and participate actively in the discussion. Utilize features like screen sharing and file sharing to enhance collaboration and ensure that all participants have access to relevant materials.

In conclusion, video conferencing and virtual meetings have become essential tools in today's business environment. By leveraging these technologies effectively, employees can bridge geographical gaps, collaborate efficiently, and build stronger relationships. By following best practices and guidelines, such as investing in reliable equipment, maintaining professionalism, and encouraging engagement, businesses can maximize the benefits of video conferencing and virtual meetings.

## Project Management and Collaboration Software

In today's fast-paced business environment, effective collaboration and project management are essential for success. With the rise of remote work and global teams, it has become increasingly important to have the right tools and strategies in place to facilitate effective communication, task management, and collaboration. This is where project management and collaboration software comes into play.

Project management and collaboration software are powerful tools that can streamline communication, enhance productivity, and ensure the successful completion of projects. These software solutions provide employees with a centralized platform to plan, execute, and monitor projects, allowing for seamless collaboration and efficient task management.

One of the key benefits of project management and collaboration software is its ability to keep everyone on the same page. With these tools, employees can easily access project timelines, task lists, and shared documents, eliminating the need for lengthy email chains or confusing back-and-forth conversations. This not only saves time but also reduces the risk of miscommunication and ensures that everyone is working towards the same goal.

Moreover, project management and collaboration software offer features that promote collaboration and teamwork. With tools such as real-time messaging, video conferencing, and document sharing, employees can collaborate effortlessly, regardless of their physical location. This is particularly important in today's business environment, where teams are often spread across different time zones and geographies.

Additionally, project management and collaboration software provide valuable insights and analytics that can help businesses make data-driven decisions. These tools allow managers to track progress, identify bottlenecks, and allocate resources effectively. By having access to real-time data and reports, businesses can improve their efficiency, optimize their workflows, and deliver projects on time and within budget.

Overall, project management and collaboration software play a crucial role in enhancing productivity, promoting effective communication, and ensuring the successful completion of projects in today's business environment. By leveraging these tools, employees can work more efficiently, collaborate seamlessly, and achieve their goals with greater ease. Whether working in the office or remotely, project management and collaboration software are indispensable assets for any business striving for success in the modern world.

## Social Media for Professional Communication

In today's fast-paced business environment, social media has become an indispensable tool for effective professional communication. It has revolutionized the way employees interact, collaborate, and exchange information, making it easier than ever to build relationships and stay connected in the business world.

One of the primary advantages of using social media in a professional setting is its ability to facilitate instant and real-time communication. Platforms such as LinkedIn, Twitter, and Slack enable employees to connect with colleagues, industry experts, and potential clients within seconds. These platforms provide an opportunity to share ideas, seek advice, and discuss industry trends, all of which can significantly enhance collaboration and knowledge-sharing in the workplace.

In addition to its speed and convenience, social media offers a cost-effective means of communication. Traditional methods like phone calls and face-to-face meetings can be time-consuming and expensive, especially in a global business environment. Social media eliminates these barriers by providing a virtual space for employees to engage in discussions and share information, regardless of their geographical location. This not only saves time and money but also promotes inclusivity and diversity within organizations.

Another crucial aspect of social media for professional communication is personal branding. Social media platforms offer employees an opportunity to showcase their expertise, skills, and achievements to a wider audience. By creating a professional online presence, employees can enhance their visibility, build credibility, and attract potential employers or clients. LinkedIn, for instance, allows individuals to create detailed profiles highlighting their professional experiences, education, and endorsements, making it an invaluable tool for networking and career advancement.

However, it is important to note that while social media offers numerous benefits, it also comes with some challenges. Employees must be mindful of their online behavior and ensure that their posts and interactions align with their company's values and professionalism. It is essential to strike a balance between personal and professional content to maintain a positive online reputation.

In conclusion, social media has become an indispensable tool for professional communication in today's business environment. Its speed, convenience, cost-effectiveness, and personal branding opportunities make it a valuable resource for employees. However, it is crucial to use social media responsibly and maintain a professional online presence. By mastering the art of social media for professional communication, employees can enhance collaboration, build relationships, and advance their careers in the competitive business world.

# Chapter 5: Communicating Across Cultures

**Understanding Cultural Differences in Communication**

In today's globalized business environment, effective communication is crucial for successful collaboration. However, communication can be challenging when working with colleagues from different cultural backgrounds. The ability to understand and adapt to cultural differences in communication is therefore essential for employees in the business environment.

Cultural differences can manifest in various ways, including language, non-verbal cues, and communication styles. Language barriers are among the most obvious challenges in cross-cultural communication. Employees must be aware that not everyone speaks the same language fluently, and misunderstandings can easily occur. It is important to use clear and concise language, avoiding jargon and idioms that may not be understood by all.

Non-verbal communication, such as body language and gestures, also varies across cultures. What may be considered acceptable or polite in one culture could be offensive in another. Employees should be mindful of these differences and strive to interpret non-verbal cues accurately. For example, maintaining eye contact may be seen as a sign of respect in one culture, but as aggressive behavior in another.

Communication styles can also differ significantly. Some cultures value direct and assertive communication, while others prioritize indirect and harmonious exchanges. Employees need to recognize and adapt to these communication styles to avoid misunderstandings and promote effective collaboration. It is important to be sensitive to cultural norms and adjust one's approach accordingly.

To bridge cultural differences in communication, employees should develop cultural intelligence. This involves being open-minded, empathetic, and willing to learn about different cultures. It is crucial to approach interactions with curiosity and respect, seeking to understand rather than judge. By actively listening and observing, employees can gain valuable insights into the cultural nuances of their colleagues.

Furthermore, organizations can support employees in navigating cultural differences by providing cultural diversity training. These training sessions can help employees develop cultural awareness and sensitivity, equipping them with the skills necessary for effective cross-cultural communication.

In conclusion, understanding and adapting to cultural differences in communication is vital in the business environment. By recognizing language barriers, interpreting non-verbal cues correctly, and adjusting communication styles, employees can foster effective collaboration with colleagues from diverse cultural backgrounds. Developing cultural intelligence and participating in cultural diversity training can further enhance employees' ability to navigate cross-cultural communication successfully. Ultimately, mastering cultural differences in communication is an essential skill for employees seeking to thrive in today's globalized business world.

## Cross-Cultural Communication Challenges

In today's globalized business environment, the ability to effectively communicate across cultures is increasingly vital for employees at all levels. As companies expand their operations internationally and engage with diverse partners, understanding and navigating cross-cultural communication challenges is essential for successful collaboration and business growth.

One of the main challenges in cross-cultural communication is the existence of different communication styles and norms. Cultures vary in terms of their preferred communication patterns, including directness, indirectness, and nonverbal cues. For example, some cultures value direct and assertive communication, while others prioritize indirect and harmonious communication. These differences can lead to misunderstandings, confusion, and even conflicts if not properly addressed.

Language barriers also pose significant challenges in cross-cultural communication. Even if employees speak a common language, nuances, idioms, and cultural references can easily be misinterpreted. Misunderstandings can lead to delays, errors, and even damage to business relationships. Therefore, it is crucial for employees to enhance their language skills and develop cultural sensitivity to bridge these gaps effectively.

Cultural differences in nonverbal communication can further complicate cross-cultural interactions. Gestures, body language, and even personal space preferences can vary significantly across cultures. For instance, what may be considered a friendly gesture in one culture could be offensive or inappropriate in another. Employees need to be aware of these differences and adapt their nonverbal cues accordingly to avoid misunderstandings and ensure effective communication.

Another challenge is the varying perceptions of time and punctuality. Some cultures place a high value on punctuality and efficiency, while others prioritize relationship-building and flexibility. These differences can lead to frustration and tension if not understood and respected. Employees should be prepared to adapt their schedules and expectations to accommodate different cultural perspectives on time management.

To overcome these challenges, employees must develop intercultural competence. This includes developing an understanding and appreciation of different cultural norms, values, and communication styles. Training programs, workshops, and cultural immersion experiences can help employees enhance their cross-cultural communication skills and become more effective collaborators in the global business environment.

By acknowledging and addressing cross-cultural communication challenges, employees can foster stronger relationships, build trust, and navigate the complexities of the business world. Mastering cross-cultural communication is not only crucial for personal and professional growth but also for the success of businesses operating in today's interconnected global marketplace.

## Strategies for Effective Communication with International Colleagues

In today's globalized business environment, effective communication with international colleagues has become a vital skill for employees. The ability to collaborate and communicate across cultures is essential for building successful partnerships, driving innovation, and achieving business goals. This subchapter explores various strategies that can help employees master the art of communication in a diverse and globalized business world.

1. Cultural Awareness: Understanding cultural differences is the first step towards effective communication. Employees should invest time in learning about the customs, traditions, and communication styles of their international colleagues. This knowledge will enable them to adapt their communication approach and avoid misunderstandings.

2. Language Skills: While it may not be possible to become fluent in every language, learning basic greetings and key phrases in the native language of international colleagues shows respect and helps in building rapport. Employees can also rely on translation tools and language assistance apps to communicate more effectively.

3. Active Listening: Listening is a crucial aspect of effective communication. Employees should practice active listening by paying attention to both verbal and non-verbal cues. They should demonstrate interest, ask clarifying questions, and seek to understand the perspective of their international colleagues.

4. Clear and Concise Communication: Communicating clearly and concisely is essential when working with international colleagues.

Employees should use simple language, avoid jargon, and break complex ideas into smaller, more digestible pieces. Visual aids, such as diagrams or presentations, can also enhance understanding.

5. Adaptability: Flexibility and adaptability are key traits when communicating with international colleagues. Employees should be open to different communication styles and be willing to adapt their own approach. This includes adapting to different time zones, scheduling meetings at convenient times, and being patient with language barriers.

6. Technology and Tools: Utilizing technology and collaboration tools can enhance communication across borders. Employees should leverage video conferencing, project management software, and instant messaging platforms to facilitate real-time communication and collaboration.

7. Respect and Empathy: Finally, showing respect and empathy towards international colleagues is crucial for building strong relationships. Employees should be mindful of cultural norms, avoid making assumptions, and demonstrate understanding and acceptance of different perspectives.

By implementing these strategies, employees can enhance their communication skills with international colleagues, resulting in improved collaboration, increased productivity, and greater success in the global business environment. Mastering effective communication across cultures is a valuable asset that can open doors to new opportunities and foster long-lasting professional relationships.

# Respecting and Appreciating Diversity in the Workplace

In today's rapidly changing business environment, diversity has become a key aspect of corporate culture. Organizations are recognizing the value and benefits of having a diverse workforce, which includes individuals from different backgrounds, cultures, races, genders, ages, and abilities. As employees in this dynamic business environment, it is crucial for us to understand the importance of respecting and appreciating diversity in the workplace.

Respecting diversity means acknowledging and accepting the differences that exist among our colleagues. It requires us to embrace various perspectives, experiences, and ideas, which can lead to innovation, creativity, and improved problem-solving. By fostering an inclusive environment, we create a platform for each employee to contribute their unique talents and skills, ultimately driving the success of our organization.

Appreciating diversity goes beyond mere tolerance; it involves actively valuing and celebrating the differences that each individual brings to the table. By appreciating diversity, we build stronger relationships, enhance teamwork, and create a positive work environment that inspires collaboration and productivity. It also helps us to develop cultural competence, enabling us to engage effectively with clients, customers, and partners from diverse backgrounds.

To effectively respect and appreciate diversity in the workplace, we must cultivate certain attitudes and behaviors. First and foremost, we should approach every interaction with an open mind, free from prejudice or biases. By being aware of our own biases and challenging them, we can create a more inclusive workplace where everyone feels valued and respected.

Active listening is another essential skill to develop. By genuinely listening to our colleagues, we can understand their perspectives, experiences, and needs better. This not only fosters empathy but also helps us generate innovative ideas and solutions by incorporating diverse viewpoints.

Furthermore, we should actively seek opportunities to learn about different cultures, traditions, and ways of thinking. This can be achieved through training programs, workshops, or simply engaging in open conversations with colleagues from diverse backgrounds. By expanding our knowledge and understanding, we can break down barriers, build trust, and foster a more inclusive and harmonious work environment.

In conclusion, respecting and appreciating diversity in the workplace is not only a moral imperative but also a critical element for success in today's business environment. By embracing diversity, we can tap into the full potential of our colleagues, foster innovation, and create a culture of inclusivity that benefits both individuals and the organization as a whole. Let us commit to promoting respect and appreciation for diversity in our workplace, and together we can create a truly collaborative and thriving business environment.

# Chapter 6: Delivering Effective Presentations

## Planning and Structuring a Presentation

Effective communication is crucial in today's fast-paced business environment. Whether you are presenting a new idea, sharing important information, or persuading your audience, mastering the art of presentation is key to achieving your goals. This subchapter titled "Planning and Structuring a Presentation" will provide you with valuable techniques and strategies to enhance your presentation skills and make a lasting impact in the business environment.

Planning a presentation is the foundation of its success. It involves understanding your audience, setting clear objectives, and organizing your content in a logical and engaging manner. Knowing your audience allows you to tailor your message to their needs, interests, and level of expertise. By doing so, you can capture their attention and ensure that your presentation is relevant and meaningful to them.

Setting clear objectives is essential to keep your presentation focused. Define what you want to achieve through your presentation – whether it is to inform, persuade, or inspire. Once your objectives are clear, you can structure your presentation accordingly, ensuring that each section and slide contributes to the overall purpose.

When structuring your presentation, a well-known technique is the "Introduction-Body-Conclusion" format. Start with a compelling introduction that grabs your audience's attention and establishes the context for your topic. The body of your presentation should provide supporting evidence, examples, and key messages. Use visuals, such as charts or graphs, to enhance understanding and retention. Finally, conclude by summarizing your main points and leaving your audience with a memorable takeaway or call to action.

In addition to the structure, consider incorporating storytelling techniques to engage your audience emotionally and make your message more memorable. Humans are wired to connect with stories, so using narratives or real-life examples can make your presentation relatable and impactful.

Lastly, rehearsing your presentation is crucial for ensuring a smooth and confident delivery. Practice your timing, tone, and body language to enhance your overall presence. Rehearsing also allows you to anticipate potential questions or challenges from your audience, enabling you to respond effectively.

In conclusion, planning and structuring a presentation is essential for effective communication in the business environment. By understanding your audience, setting clear objectives, and organizing your content in a logical and engaging manner, you can deliver a presentation that captivates your audience and achieves your desired outcomes. Remember to incorporate storytelling techniques and rehearse your delivery to make a lasting impact. Mastering the art of presentation will undoubtedly enhance your collaboration and success in the business world.

## Engaging Your Audience

In today's fast-paced business environment, effective communication is paramount to achieving success. As employees, it is crucial to master the art of engaging your audience to ensure effective collaboration and build strong professional relationships. This subchapter of "Mastering Business Communication: Techniques for Effective Collaboration" will provide you with valuable insights and techniques to captivate your audience and deliver your message with impact.

The first step in engaging your audience is to understand their needs, interests, and preferences. Take the time to research and analyze your audience before any interaction or presentation. By doing so, you can tailor your message to resonate with their specific concerns and objectives. This will not only help you capture their attention but also establish credibility and trust.

Next, it is essential to use clear and concise language to convey your ideas. Avoid jargon or technical terms that may confuse or alienate your audience. Instead, use plain language that is easy to understand, ensuring that your message is accessible to everyone. Additionally, consider using visuals such as charts, graphs, or infographics to supplement your communication and make it more engaging and memorable.

Another powerful technique for engaging your audience is storytelling. Humans have been telling stories for centuries, and they continue to be a compelling way to captivate attention and convey complex ideas. Incorporate relevant anecdotes or case studies into your communication to make it relatable and memorable. By connecting on an emotional level, you can create a lasting impact and enhance audience engagement.

Active listening is also vital in engaging your audience. Encourage dialogue and ask open-ended questions to involve your audience in the conversation. Show genuine interest in their opinions and perspectives, and be responsive to their feedback. This fosters a collaborative environment where everyone feels valued, leading to enhanced engagement and productive outcomes.

Lastly, embrace technology as a tool to engage your audience. Utilize interactive platforms, such as online surveys or virtual collaboration tools, to encourage participation and gather feedback. Embracing new technologies shows your commitment to staying relevant and adapting to the ever-evolving business landscape.

In conclusion, engaging your audience is a fundamental skill in the dynamic business environment. By understanding their needs, using clear language, leveraging storytelling techniques, actively listening, and embracing technology, you can create impactful communication that drives collaboration and success. Apply these techniques consistently, and you will become a master of engaging your audience, fostering strong professional relationships, and achieving your business objectives.

## Visual Aids and Presentation Tools

In today's dynamic business environment, effective communication has become a critical skill for employees across all industries. Whether you are delivering a presentation to clients, colleagues, or superiors, the ability to convey your message clearly and persuasively is essential. Visual aids and presentation tools play a vital role in enhancing your communication skills and ensuring that your message is delivered effectively.

Visual aids, such as slides, charts, graphs, and images, can help you present complex information in a concise and visually appealing manner. They provide a powerful tool to engage your audience and capture their attention. By using visuals, you can break down complex concepts into simple, easy-to-understand graphics, making it easier for your audience to grasp and retain information.

One of the most popular presentation tools used in the business environment is Microsoft PowerPoint. With its user-friendly interface and extensive range of features, PowerPoint allows you to create professional-looking presentations with ease. You can customize the design, layout, and colors to match your branding or corporate identity. Additionally, PowerPoint enables you to incorporate various media elements, such as videos and audio clips, to make your presentations more dynamic and interactive.

Aside from PowerPoint, there are other presentation tools available that cater to specific needs. For instance, Prezi offers a unique zooming feature that allows you to create engaging, non-linear presentations. Keynote, on the other hand, is a popular choice for

Apple users, offering sleek design options and seamless integration with other Apple devices.

When using visual aids and presentation tools, it is crucial to remember a few key principles. Firstly, keep your slides or visuals simple and uncluttered. Avoid overcrowding them with excessive text or complicated graphics. Instead, use bullet points or concise statements to convey your main ideas. Secondly, make sure your visuals are visually appealing and aligned with your overall message. Choose colors, fonts, and images that are consistent with your brand and enhance the visual impact of your presentation.

Lastly, practice your presentation beforehand to ensure a smooth delivery. Familiarize yourself with the tools and features of your chosen presentation software, and rehearse your speech to build confidence. Remember to maintain eye contact with your audience and use your visuals as supporting aids rather than relying on them entirely.

In conclusion, visual aids and presentation tools are indispensable in today's business environment. They provide employees with the means to deliver engaging and compelling presentations. By using tools like PowerPoint, Prezi, or Keynote, employees can enhance their communication skills and effectively convey their message to their audience. By following key principles, such as simplicity, visual appeal, and practice, employees can master the art of using visual aids and presentation tools to their advantage in the business world.

## Overcoming Stage Fright and Nervousness

Introduction

In the fast-paced and competitive business environment, effective communication is crucial for success. Whether you are presenting to a small team or a large audience, stage fright and nervousness can hinder your ability to convey your message effectively. However, with the right techniques and mindset, you can overcome these challenges and become a confident and persuasive communicator. This subchapter will explore practical strategies to help employees in the business environment conquer stage fright and nervousness.

Understanding                                    Stage                                    Fright

Stage fright is a common phenomenon that affects even the most experienced individuals. It is important to recognize that feeling nervous before a presentation is natural. However, excessive anxiety can impair your performance and undermine your credibility. By understanding the root causes of stage fright, you can better address and manage it.

Preparation                                    is                                    Key

One of the most effective ways to combat stage fright is through thorough preparation. Practice your presentation multiple times, familiarizing yourself with the content and flow. This will boost your confidence and reduce anxiety. Additionally, rehearsing in front of a mirror or with a trusted colleague can help simulate the experience of speaking in front of others.

Visualize                                    Success

Visualization is a powerful technique that can help alleviate nervousness. Mentally rehearse your presentation going smoothly, envisioning positive reactions from the audience. By creating a mental image of success, you program your mind to believe in your capabilities and reduce anxiety.

Focus on Your Audience

Shifting your focus from your own nervousness to your audience can make a significant difference in your performance. Instead of worrying about how you appear, concentrate on delivering value to your listeners. Understand their needs, tailor your content accordingly, and engage them through interactive elements. This shift in mindset will not only diminish your stage fright but also enhance your ability to connect with your audience.

Control Your Breathing and Body Language

Deep breathing exercises before and during your presentation can help regulate your heart rate and calm your nerves. Additionally, pay attention to your body language. Stand tall, maintain eye contact, and use gestures to convey confidence and openness. These non-verbal cues can help you project assurance and reduce anxiety.

Conclusion

Overcoming stage fright and nervousness is essential for effective communication in the business environment. By understanding the causes of stage fright, preparing thoroughly, visualizing success, focusing on the audience, and controlling your breathing and body language, you can conquer your fears and deliver impactful presentations. Remember, practice makes perfect, and with time and effort, you will become a confident and influential communicator in any business setting.

# Chapter 7: Effective Business Writing

## Writing Clear and Concise Emails

In today's fast-paced business environment, effective communication is key to successful collaboration. One of the most common forms of communication in the corporate world is email. However, poorly written emails can lead to misunderstandings, wasted time, and even damage relationships. To ensure your emails are clear and concise, follow these guidelines.

1. Keep it short and to the point: In a busy business environment, people don't have time to read lengthy emails. Be direct and get to the main point quickly. Use short sentences and paragraphs to enhance readability.

2. Use a descriptive subject line: The subject line is the first thing recipients see, so make it informative and specific. It should highlight the main purpose or topic of the email, allowing recipients to prioritize and respond accordingly.

3. Start with a polite and concise greeting: Begin your email with a professional greeting such as "Dear [Recipient's Name]," or a simple "Hello." Avoid informal or overly casual language.

4. Organize your content logically: Structure your email in a way that is easy to follow. Use headings or bullet points to break down complex information into manageable sections. This helps recipients quickly locate the information they need.

5. Be clear and specific in your message: Clearly state the purpose or intention of your email in the first few sentences. Avoid ambiguity or vague language that may confuse the recipient. Use specific and concrete examples to support your points.

6. Use proper grammar and punctuation: Poor grammar and punctuation can make your email appear unprofessional and may lead to misunderstandings. Proofread your email before sending it to ensure it is error-free.

7. Avoid unnecessary jargon or acronyms: While industry-specific terms may be familiar to you, they may confuse recipients outside your niche. Use plain language that can be easily understood by anyone.

8. Proofread and revise your email: Before hitting the send button, take a moment to review your email. Check for any spelling or grammatical errors, and ensure your message is concise and clear.

Remember, writing clear and concise emails not only saves time but also enhances your professional image. By following these guidelines, you can ensure that your emails are effective, professional, and well-received in the business environment.

## Crafting Professional Memos and Reports

In today's fast-paced and competitive business environment, effective communication is paramount for success. One of the essential skills that employees need to master is crafting professional memos and reports. Whether you are communicating internally within your organization or externally with clients and stakeholders, the ability to convey information in a clear, concise, and professional manner is crucial.

This subchapter aims to provide employees in the business environment with practical techniques and strategies to enhance their memo and report writing skills. By following these guidelines, you will be able to create documents that effectively communicate your ideas, proposals, and recommendations.

To start, it is important to understand the purpose and audience of your memo or report. Clearly define your objectives and tailor your communication to meet the specific needs of your readers. Consider their level of expertise, their expectations, and their preferred style of communication. This will help you structure your content and select the appropriate tone and language.

The next step is to organize your thoughts and information logically. Begin with a concise executive summary or introduction that provides an overview of the main points. Use headings and subheadings to break down complex information into manageable sections. This will make it easier for your audience to navigate and understand your document.

When writing, strive for clarity and brevity. Use plain language and avoid unnecessary jargon or technical terms that may confuse your readers. Keep your sentences and paragraphs concise, allowing for easy readability. Use bullet points or numbered lists when appropriate to present information in a clear and organized manner.

In addition to clarity, ensure that your memo or report is professional in tone and appearance. Use a professional font and formatting style, and proofread your document carefully for any grammatical or spelling errors. Pay attention to the overall structure, including headings, subheadings, and visual elements such as tables or graphs, to enhance readability and comprehension.

Lastly, consider the action you want your readers to take after reading your memo or report. Include a clear call to action or next steps to ensure that your communication has a purpose and leads to tangible outcomes.

By mastering the art of crafting professional memos and reports, employees in the business environment can effectively collaborate, make informed decisions, and drive results. These skills are essential for success in today's fast-paced and highly competitive business landscape.

## Writing for Different Business Purposes (Marketing, Sales, etc.)

In today's dynamic business environment, effective communication is key to success. Whether you are an employee, a manager, or an entrepreneur, the ability to write for different business purposes is crucial. This subchapter will explore the various writing styles and techniques required in marketing, sales, and other business-related activities.

Marketing is a crucial aspect of any business. It is the art of promoting products or services to customers and building brand awareness. When it comes to writing for marketing purposes, creativity and persuasion are essential. Your goal is to engage and capture the attention of your target audience. This requires crafting compelling content that showcases the unique selling points of your product or service. Utilize persuasive language, storytelling techniques, and emotional appeal to create a memorable and impactful marketing message.

Sales writing, on the other hand, is focused on closing deals and generating revenue. It requires a more direct and persuasive approach. Your writing should highlight the benefits of your product or service and convince potential customers of its value. Use clear and concise language to convey your message, and provide relevant information that addresses the needs and concerns of your target market. Additionally, incorporating testimonials and case studies can strengthen your sales pitch and build trust with potential customers.

In addition to marketing and sales, there are various other business purposes that require effective writing skills. These include writing business proposals, reports, emails, and memos. Each of these writing tasks requires a different approach and style. When writing business proposals, for example, you need to be concise, persuasive, and organized. Your goal is to convince potential clients or stakeholders that your proposal is the best solution to their needs.

When it comes to writing emails and memos, clarity and professionalism are key. Keep your messages concise and to the point, and ensure that your tone is appropriate for the recipient. Pay attention to grammar and spelling, as a well-written email or memo reflects positively on your professionalism and attention to detail.

In conclusion, mastering the art of writing for different business purposes is essential in today's business environment. Whether you are involved in marketing, sales, or any other aspect of business, effective communication can make all the difference. By understanding the specific requirements and techniques for each purpose, you can enhance your writing skills and achieve greater success in your professional endeavors.

## Proofreading and Editing Techniques

Proofreading and editing are essential skills in the business environment that can greatly enhance communication and collaboration. Whether you are drafting an important email, creating a presentation, or preparing a report, it is crucial to ensure that your written content is error-free and effectively conveys your intended message. In this subchapter, we will explore some useful proofreading and editing techniques that will help employees master the art of business communication.

The first step in the proofreading process is to review your content for grammar, spelling, and punctuation errors. This can be done by carefully reading through the entire document, sentence by sentence, and correcting any mistakes you come across. Pay close attention to commonly confused words, such as "their" and "there," and ensure that your sentences are properly structured and punctuated.

Another important technique is to read your content aloud. This helps in identifying awkward sentence structures, repetitive phrases, and unclear ideas. By hearing your words, you can better gauge how your message will be perceived by others and make necessary revisions to improve clarity and coherence.

Additionally, it is crucial to review your content for consistency. Check that your formatting, font styles, and headings are consistent throughout the document. Ensure that any abbreviations or acronyms are spelled out or defined upon first use. Consistency in formatting and terminology helps maintain a professional and polished appearance.

When editing, it is essential to keep your audience in mind. Consider the knowledge and expertise of your intended readers and adjust your language and vocabulary accordingly. Avoid jargon and technical terms if they may be unfamiliar to your audience, and strive for a tone that is professional, yet approachable.

Lastly, always seek feedback from others. Ask a colleague or supervisor to review your work and provide constructive criticism. Fresh eyes can catch errors or suggest improvements that you may have missed. Actively seek feedback and be open to making revisions based on the input you receive.

By implementing these proofreading and editing techniques, employees can ensure that their written communication is error-free, coherent, and effectively conveys their intended message. Improving these skills will not only enhance internal collaboration but also establish a professional image for your organization in the business environment.

# Chapter 8: Effective Communication in Leadership Roles

## Communicating Vision and Goals

In today's fast-paced and competitive business environment, effective communication plays a crucial role in the success of any organization. As employees, it is essential to understand the vision and goals of the company we work for, as this knowledge empowers us to align our efforts and contribute towards achieving these objectives. This subchapter explores the importance of communicating vision and goals within the business environment and provides techniques for effective collaboration.

A clear and compelling vision serves as a guiding light for an organization. It encapsulates the purpose, values, and aspirations of the company, inspiring employees to work towards a common goal. By effectively communicating the vision, employees gain a sense of direction, motivation, and a deeper understanding of their role in the bigger picture. When everyone is on the same page, collaboration and teamwork improve, leading to increased productivity and success.

To effectively communicate the vision and goals, it is crucial to use various channels and mediums. Leaders should not rely solely on emails or memos but should also engage in face-to-face interactions, town hall meetings, or video conferences to ensure clarity and understanding. Visual aids, such as presentations or infographics, can also be used to enhance comprehension and engagement.

Furthermore, employees should have a clear understanding of the goals set by the organization. These goals provide a roadmap for success and help employees prioritize their tasks and efforts. Regular updates and progress reports should be shared to keep everyone informed about the progress towards these goals. This transparency fosters a sense of accountability and encourages employees to take ownership of their work.

In addition to communication, active listening is a crucial skill for employees. By actively listening to the vision and goals communicated by leaders, employees can ask questions, seek clarification, and provide valuable feedback. This two-way communication promotes a culture of trust, collaboration, and innovation.

In conclusion, communicating vision and goals is vital for employees in the business environment. It aligns everyone towards a common purpose, enhances collaboration, and improves productivity. By using diverse communication channels, providing regular updates, and actively listening, organizations can ensure that their employees are well-informed and motivated to contribute towards achieving the vision and goals of the company.

## Providing Constructive Feedback

In any business environment, effective communication is key to achieving success and maintaining strong collaboration among employees. One essential aspect of effective communication is providing constructive feedback. This subchapter aims to equip employees with the necessary knowledge and techniques to deliver feedback that promotes growth and improvement, fostering a positive work environment.

Constructive feedback is a valuable tool that helps individuals identify their strengths and areas for improvement. By offering feedback in a constructive manner, employees can inspire growth, boost morale, and enhance overall performance. Here are some essential techniques to consider when providing constructive feedback:

1. Be specific and objective: When delivering feedback, it is crucial to focus on specific behaviors or actions rather than making generalizations. By providing concrete examples and avoiding personal judgments, employees can better understand the areas they need to work on.

2. Use the feedback sandwich approach: The feedback sandwich approach involves starting with positive feedback, followed by constructive criticism, and concluding with positive reinforcement. This technique helps balance the negative aspects with encouragement, making the feedback more palatable and motivating.

3. Focus on future improvement: Instead of dwelling on past mistakes, emphasize how employees can learn from them and move forward. By

discussing specific strategies or resources for improvement, employees will feel supported and motivated to enhance their skills.

4. Encourage self-reflection: Instead of only providing feedback, encourage employees to reflect on their own performance. This self-reflection allows individuals to take ownership of their growth and development, fostering a sense of accountability.

5. Active listening: When providing constructive feedback, it is essential to actively listen to employees' concerns or questions. By showing empathy and understanding, employees will feel valued and more inclined to accept and act upon the feedback.

By implementing these techniques, employees can effectively provide constructive feedback that promotes growth and fosters a positive work environment. It is important to remember that constructive feedback should be an ongoing process, rather than a one-time event. Regular check-ins and open communication channels will ensure continuous improvement and collaboration among employees.

Mastering the art of providing constructive feedback is a valuable skill that can enhance individual and team performance in any business environment. By following these techniques, employees can contribute to a culture of open communication, growth, and success within their organization.

**Motivating and Inspiring Your Team**

In today's fast-paced and competitive business environment, it is crucial for employees to feel motivated and inspired to give their best. As an employee, you play a vital role in not only your own success but also in fostering a positive and productive work environment. This subchapter will provide you with valuable techniques and strategies to motivate and inspire your team, ultimately leading to increased collaboration and success in the business environment.

1. Lead by example: One of the most effective ways to motivate and inspire your team is by leading by example. Show dedication, enthusiasm, and a strong work ethic in your own tasks and responsibilities. Your passion and commitment will inspire your colleagues to do the same.

2. Recognize and appreciate: Everyone loves to be recognized and appreciated for their hard work. Take the time to acknowledge your team members' achievements and efforts. This can be done through verbal recognition, written appreciation notes, or even small gestures like treating them to lunch. By valuing their contributions, you create a positive and motivating atmosphere.

3. Set clear goals and expectations: To motivate your team, provide them with clear goals and expectations. When employees understand what is expected of them, they can work towards achieving those targets. Regularly communicate progress and provide feedback to keep everyone on track and motivated.

4. Foster open communication: Encourage open communication within your team. When employees feel comfortable expressing their

ideas, concerns, and suggestions, it promotes a sense of belonging and ownership. Actively listen to your team members and consider their input. This will not only motivate them but also lead to innovation and collaboration.

5. Offer growth and development opportunities: Motivate your team by providing growth and development opportunities. This can be in the form of training programs, workshops, or mentoring. When employees see that the organization is invested in their personal and professional growth, it inspires them to perform at their best.

6. Celebrate achievements: Celebrate team achievements and milestones. Whether it's completing a challenging project or surpassing a target, recognizing and celebrating success boosts morale and motivates your team to aim for greater accomplishments.

Remember, motivating and inspiring your team is an ongoing process. It requires consistent effort and genuine care for your colleagues' well-being and growth. By implementing these techniques, you can create a positive and collaborative work environment where everyone feels motivated to excel in the dynamic business environment.

## Leading Effective Meetings

In today's fast-paced business environment, meetings have become an integral part of our professional lives. Whether it is a team huddle, a project update, or a brainstorming session, meetings play a crucial role in collaboration and decision-making. However, all too often, meetings can be unproductive and time-consuming, leaving employees feeling frustrated and drained. To ensure that meetings are efficient and fruitful, it is essential to master the art of leading effective meetings.

In this subchapter, we will explore various techniques and strategies that will empower employees to lead successful meetings. From planning and preparation to facilitation and follow-up, every aspect of conducting a meeting will be covered.

The first step to leading effective meetings is thorough planning. This involves setting clear objectives, creating an agenda, and identifying the necessary participants. By clearly defining the purpose and desired outcomes of the meeting, employees can ensure that everyone is on the same page and that time is utilized effectively.

Next, we delve into the art of facilitation. An effective meeting leader knows how to engage participants, encourage collaboration, and manage time efficiently. Techniques such as active listening, encouraging participation, and summarizing key points will be explored in detail, equipping employees with the tools they need to create a positive and productive meeting environment.

Furthermore, this subchapter emphasizes the importance of effective communication during meetings. From delivering concise presentations to asking open-ended questions, employees will learn how to convey information clearly and engage others in meaningful discussions.

Finally, we address the critical aspect of follow-up. Many meetings fail to achieve their intended goals because action items are not properly documented or followed through. Employees will be provided with practical tips for documenting meeting minutes, assigning tasks, and monitoring progress, ensuring that the outcomes of the meeting are implemented effectively.

By mastering the techniques outlined in this subchapter, employees will be equipped with the skills necessary to lead effective meetings in the dynamic business environment. Improved meeting efficiency will not only save valuable time but also enhance collaboration, foster innovation, and ultimately contribute to the overall success of the organization.

# Chapter 9: Communication in Remote and Virtual Work Environments

## Overcoming Communication Challenges in Remote Work

In today's fast-paced business environment, remote work has become increasingly popular. With the advancements in technology and the changing dynamics of the workforce, it is now common for employees to collaborate and communicate with their colleagues and clients from different locations. However, while remote work offers numerous benefits, it also presents unique communication challenges that employees must overcome to ensure effective collaboration.

One of the main challenges faced in remote work is the lack of face-to-face interaction. Traditional communication methods such as phone calls and emails may not always be sufficient to convey ideas and emotions accurately. Misinterpretations and misunderstandings can easily arise, leading to delays in projects and a breakdown in communication. To overcome this challenge, employees must utilize video conferencing tools to facilitate virtual meetings and discussions. By incorporating visual cues and body language, employees can enhance understanding and build stronger connections with their team members.

Another significant communication challenge in remote work is the difficulty in establishing trust and rapport. In a physical office setting, employees have the advantage of casual conversations and social interactions that contribute to building relationships. In a remote work environment, employees need to make a conscious effort to foster connections with their colleagues. Regular check-ins, virtual team-building activities, and open communication channels can help bridge the gap and create a sense of camaraderie among team members.

Additionally, remote work often involves working across different time zones, making synchronous communication challenging. To overcome this obstacle, employees should embrace asynchronous communication tools such as project management software and instant messaging platforms. These tools allow for effective collaboration and information sharing, regardless of time differences. By establishing clear guidelines on response times and expectations, employees can maintain efficient communication and ensure that everyone is on the same page.

Lastly, remote work can sometimes lead to feelings of isolation and disengagement. Without the physical presence of colleagues, employees may struggle to stay motivated and connected to the organization. To address this challenge, employers should encourage regular team meetings, provide opportunities for social interactions, and celebrate achievements as a team. Employees should also take proactive steps to stay engaged, such as establishing a dedicated workspace, setting clear boundaries between work and personal life, and seeking support from colleagues and mentors.

In conclusion, while remote work offers flexibility and freedom, it also poses unique communication challenges in the business environment. By utilizing video conferencing, fostering trust and rapport, embracing asynchronous communication tools, and combating feelings of isolation, employees can overcome these challenges and ensure effective collaboration in the remote work setting.

## Building Trust and Connection in Virtual Teams

In today's fast-paced business environment, virtual teams have become increasingly common. With the rise of technology and globalization, employees are often required to work collaboratively with colleagues from different locations and time zones. However, building trust and connection in virtual teams can be challenging, as face-to-face interactions are limited. This subchapter explores effective techniques for fostering trust and connection in virtual teams, enabling employees to collaborate more effectively and achieve their goals.

One of the key aspects of building trust in virtual teams is communication. Regular and open communication is crucial to ensure that team members feel connected and informed. Utilizing various communication tools such as video conferencing, email, and instant messaging can help bridge the gap and create a sense of presence. Encouraging team members to share their thoughts and ideas openly fosters a collaborative environment and builds trust among team members.

Another important element in building trust is setting clear expectations. Clearly defining roles, responsibilities, and deadlines helps to establish accountability and reliability within the team. When team members understand what is expected of them, they can work towards common goals more efficiently. Regular check-ins and progress updates also help to ensure that everyone is on the same page and align their efforts.

Trust can also be built through virtual team-building activities. Engaging in team-building exercises, even in a virtual setting, can help team members get to know each other on a personal level. This can include virtual icebreakers, online games, or even sharing personal stories. Building personal connections within the team enhances trust and creates a more supportive and collaborative work environment.

In addition to these techniques, it is essential to promote a culture of respect and inclusivity within virtual teams. Encouraging active listening, valuing diverse perspectives, and fostering a supportive atmosphere are crucial to building trust and connection. When team members feel respected and valued, they are more likely to trust each other and work together effectively.

In conclusion, building trust and connection in virtual teams is essential for effective collaboration in today's business environment. By focusing on open communication, setting clear expectations, engaging in team-building activities, and promoting a culture of respect, employees can foster trust and connection within their virtual teams. By doing so, they can overcome the challenges of virtual collaboration and achieve success together.

## Effective Communication in a Digital Workplace

In today's fast-paced business environment, the digital workplace has become the norm. With the advancement of technology and the rise of remote work, effective communication has become more crucial than ever. In this subchapter, we will explore the techniques and strategies for mastering communication in a digital workplace.

1. Embrace Digital Tools: The digital workplace offers a plethora of communication tools such as email, instant messaging, video conferencing, and collaboration platforms. Familiarize yourself with these tools and utilize them effectively to ensure seamless communication with your colleagues, superiors, and clients.

2. Be Clear and Concise: In a digital workplace, messages can easily be misinterpreted. Therefore, it is essential to communicate your thoughts clearly and concisely. Use short sentences, bullet points, and headings to make your message easily scannable and understandable.

3. Active Listening: Communication is a two-way process, and active listening plays a crucial role in effective communication. Pay attention to what others are saying, ask clarifying questions, and provide thoughtful responses. This will not only foster better understanding but also demonstrate your engagement and commitment to the conversation.

4. Use Visuals: In a digital environment, visual aids can enhance communication and make complex information more accessible. Incorporate graphs, charts, and infographics to convey your message effectively and engage your audience. Visuals can break down barriers and facilitate better comprehension.

5. Be Mindful of Tone: Without the ability to see facial expressions or hear vocal tone, written messages can easily be misinterpreted. Be mindful of your tone and choose words carefully to avoid misunderstandings. Use emoticons or emojis sparingly to convey your emotions, but remember to maintain professionalism.

6. Timely Responses: In a digital workplace, responsiveness is crucial. Aim to respond to messages and emails promptly, even if it's just to acknowledge receipt. This shows respect for others' time and ensures efficient collaboration.

7. Foster Relationships: Building relationships in a digital workplace can be challenging, but it is essential for effective communication. Take the initiative to connect with colleagues through virtual coffee breaks or team-building activities. Engage in non-work-related conversations to foster rapport and strengthen bonds.

In conclusion, effective communication in a digital workplace is vital for successful collaboration in today's business environment. By embracing digital tools, being clear and concise, actively listening, using visuals, being mindful of tone, providing timely responses, and fostering relationships, employees can enhance their communication skills and thrive in a digital workplace. Mastering these techniques will not only promote effective collaboration but also contribute to personal and professional growth in the business environment.

## Maintaining Work-Life Balance in Remote Work

In today's fast-paced business environment, remote work has become increasingly popular. With the advancements in technology, employees now have the flexibility to work from anywhere, at any time. While this newfound freedom offers numerous benefits, it also poses challenges in maintaining a healthy work-life balance. In this subchapter, we will explore effective strategies for employees to navigate the remote work landscape and find harmony between their professional and personal lives.

First and foremost, it is crucial to establish clear boundaries between work and personal life. When working remotely, the line between the two can easily blur, leading to longer working hours and increased stress levels. Set specific working hours and communicate them to your colleagues and managers. Stick to these hours as much as possible, and avoid the temptation to constantly check emails or respond to work-related requests outside of this timeframe. By setting boundaries, you will be able to allocate dedicated time for personal activities, family, and self-care.

Another key aspect of maintaining work-life balance in remote work is creating a dedicated workspace. Designate a specific area in your home as your office, preferably away from distractions. This will help create a mental separation between work and personal life, allowing you to focus and be productive during working hours. Additionally, having a dedicated workspace will make it easier to "leave work" at the end of the day and transition into your personal life.

Effective communication is also vital when it comes to work-life balance in a remote setup. Clearly communicate your availability and preferred modes of communication to your colleagues and managers. By setting expectations from the beginning, you can avoid unnecessary interruptions during personal time or non-working hours. Additionally, make use of collaboration tools and project management software to streamline communication and keep track of tasks, deadlines, and progress. This will help you stay organized and minimize the risk of work encroaching into personal time.

Lastly, prioritize self-care and make time for activities that recharge and rejuvenate you. It is easy to get caught up in the demands of remote work and neglect personal well-being. Maintain a healthy work-life balance by scheduling breaks, engaging in physical exercise, practicing mindfulness, and spending quality time with loved ones. Remember, taking care of yourself is not a luxury but a necessity for long-term success and happiness.

In conclusion, while remote work offers flexibility and freedom, maintaining work-life balance is essential for employees in the business environment. By setting clear boundaries, creating a dedicated workspace, communicating effectively, and prioritizing self-care, employees can thrive in their professional and personal lives. Embracing these strategies will not only improve productivity and job satisfaction but also contribute to overall well-being and success in the remote work landscape.

# Chapter 10: Effective Negotiation and Conflict Resolution

## Understanding the Negotiation Process

Negotiation is an essential skill in the business environment. Whether you are dealing with clients, colleagues, or suppliers, the ability to negotiate effectively can lead to successful outcomes and strengthen professional relationships. This subchapter aims to provide employees with a comprehensive understanding of the negotiation process, equipping them with the tools and techniques needed to navigate through various business negotiations.

The negotiation process can be complex, involving multiple parties, differing interests, and potential conflicts. Therefore, it is crucial to approach negotiations with a strategic mindset. This subchapter will guide employees through the key stages of negotiation, starting with preparation. Before entering any negotiation, it is essential to gather information, identify goals, and assess the other party's interests. By doing so, employees can develop a clear strategy and be better positioned to achieve their desired outcomes.

Once the preparation is complete, the subchapter will delve into the negotiation techniques employees can employ during the discussion phase. It will explore the importance of active listening, effective communication, and the art of persuasion. Furthermore, it will emphasize the significance of maintaining a respectful and collaborative attitude throughout the negotiation process, fostering an environment of trust and open dialogue.

Understanding the dynamics of power is another critical aspect covered in this subchapter. Employees will learn how to identify power imbalances, leverage their own strengths, and navigate power disparities to achieve mutually beneficial agreements. Additionally, the subchapter will address the role of compromise and finding win-win solutions, emphasizing the value of maintaining positive relationships even after the negotiation has concluded.

Lastly, this subchapter will discuss the importance of evaluating and learning from each negotiation experience. By reflecting on the negotiation process, employees can identify areas for improvement and refine their negotiation skills over time. It will provide practical tips on debriefing, analyzing outcomes, and applying lessons learned to future negotiations.

Overall, "Understanding the Negotiation Process" is a subchapter that aims to equip employees in the business environment with the knowledge and skills necessary to become proficient negotiators. By mastering the negotiation process, employees can enhance their effectiveness in collaborative business settings and contribute to the overall success of their organizations.

## Effective Negotiation Techniques

Negotiation is an essential skill in today's business environment. Whether you are discussing a new project with your colleagues or closing a deal with a potential client, knowing how to negotiate effectively can make a significant difference in achieving successful outcomes. This subchapter will provide you with valuable insights and techniques that will help you become a master negotiator.

1. Preparation: Before entering into any negotiation, it is crucial to gather as much information as possible. Understand the needs, interests, and positions of all parties involved. This knowledge will enable you to make informed decisions during the negotiation process.

2. Active listening: Effective communication is at the core of successful negotiation. Actively listen to the other party's concerns, ideas, and objectives. By doing so, you show respect and create an environment of collaboration and understanding. This will ultimately lead to a win-win situation.

3. Building rapport: Establishing a positive relationship with the other party is key to successful negotiations. Find common ground and show empathy to their perspective. Building rapport will create trust and make the negotiation process smoother.

4. Setting clear objectives: Clearly define your objectives and desired outcomes before entering into a negotiation. This will help you stay focused and avoid getting sidetracked during the discussion.

5. Win-win mindset: Negotiation should not be a win-lose situation; instead, aim for a win-win outcome where both parties feel satisfied.

Focus on creating value and finding innovative solutions that meet the interests of all parties involved.

6. Effective communication: Choose your words carefully and use persuasive language to convey your ideas. Be assertive but respectful, and always maintain a professional tone. Non-verbal cues, such as body language and tone of voice, also play a significant role in effective communication during negotiations.

7. Problem-solving approach: Instead of viewing negotiation as a battleground, approach it as an opportunity to find solutions to common problems. By adopting a problem-solving mindset, you can work collaboratively with the other party to achieve mutually beneficial outcomes.

8. Patience and flexibility: Negotiation can be a time-consuming process, so it is important to remain patient and flexible. Be open to alternative ideas and be willing to compromise when necessary. This flexibility will help maintain a positive atmosphere and increase the chances of reaching an agreement.

By mastering these effective negotiation techniques, you will be able to navigate through various business scenarios with confidence and achieve favorable outcomes. Remember, negotiation is not about winning at the expense of others, but about finding common ground and creating long-lasting partnerships.

## Resolving Conflicts in the Workplace

Conflict is an inevitable part of any business environment. With different personalities, perspectives, and goals, conflicts are bound to arise. However, resolving conflicts effectively is crucial for maintaining a positive and productive work environment. In this subchapter, we will explore various techniques for resolving conflicts in the workplace, providing employees with the necessary tools to navigate and overcome these challenges.

1. Understanding Conflict: The first step in resolving conflicts is to understand their nature and causes. Conflict can stem from differences in opinions, communication breakdowns, competition for resources, or personal issues. By identifying the root cause, employees can approach conflicts with a clearer understanding and empathy towards one another.

2. Effective Communication: Communication is key when it comes to conflict resolution. Encouraging open and honest dialogue between parties involved can help uncover misunderstandings and find common ground. Active listening, expressing viewpoints respectfully, and asking clarifying questions are all essential in promoting effective communication.

3. Collaboration and Compromise: Often, conflicts arise due to conflicting interests or goals. Encouraging collaboration and finding solutions that satisfy both parties' needs can help resolve conflicts. Employees should be willing to compromise and seek win-win outcomes rather than engaging in a win-lose mentality.

4. Mediation and Conflict Resolution Techniques: In situations where conflicts escalate and parties cannot resolve them independently, seeking mediation or involving a neutral third party can be beneficial. Trained mediators can facilitate discussions, guide the process, and help parties reach a mutually acceptable solution.

5. Building Relationships: Building positive relationships in the workplace is crucial for conflict prevention and resolution. When employees have strong relationships built on trust and respect, they are more likely to address conflicts constructively and find solutions collaboratively.

6. Emotional Intelligence: Developing emotional intelligence is essential for conflict resolution. Employees should be aware of their emotions and learn to manage them effectively. Understanding others' emotions and being empathetic can also contribute to resolving conflicts more constructively.

7. Learning from Conflicts: Conflicts can provide valuable learning opportunities. After a conflict is resolved, employees should reflect on the experience and identify any lessons learned. This reflection can help prevent similar conflicts in the future and promote personal and professional growth.

By mastering the techniques for resolving conflicts in the workplace, employees can contribute to a harmonious and productive business environment. Through effective communication, collaboration, and the development of emotional intelligence, conflicts can be transformed into opportunities for growth, innovation, and stronger relationships among team members.

## Mediation and Collaborative Problem-Solving

Mediation and Collaborative Problem-Solving: Building Stronger Business Relationships

In today's fast-paced and highly competitive business environment, effective communication and problem-solving skills are crucial for success. As employees, we often find ourselves facing conflicts and challenges that require a collaborative approach to find a resolution. It is in these situations that mediation and collaborative problem-solving techniques come into play.

Mediation is a process where a neutral third party facilitates a conversation between two or more individuals who are in conflict. It provides a structured and safe environment for employees to express their concerns and work towards a mutually beneficial solution. Mediation allows for open dialogue, active listening, and the exploration of various perspectives, leading to a deeper understanding of the issues at hand.

Collaborative problem-solving, on the other hand, involves bringing together a diverse group of individuals to collectively brainstorm solutions to a common problem. This approach encourages innovative thinking, fosters teamwork, and promotes a sense of ownership and commitment to the final outcome. By leveraging the unique strengths and expertise of each team member, collaborative problem-solving can lead to more effective and sustainable solutions.

So, how can we master the art of mediation and collaborative problem-solving in the business environment?

First and foremost, it is essential to approach conflicts with an open mind and a willingness to listen. Active listening is a powerful tool that allows us to fully understand the concerns and perspectives of others. By demonstrating empathy and respect, we create an atmosphere of trust, which is crucial for successful mediation and problem-solving.

Additionally, effective communication skills, such as clear and concise verbal and written communication, are vital. Being able to articulate our thoughts and ideas in a way that is easily understood by others enables us to contribute effectively to the mediation or problem-solving process.

Furthermore, embracing a solution-oriented mindset is key. Instead of focusing on blame or past mistakes, we should shift our attention towards finding a solution that benefits all parties involved. This requires creativity, flexibility, and a willingness to explore alternative options.

Lastly, it is crucial to recognize the importance of compromise and negotiation. Mediation and collaborative problem-solving often require finding a middle ground that satisfies the needs and interests of all parties. By engaging in constructive dialogue and seeking common ground, we can reach agreements that are fair and sustainable.

In conclusion, mastering the techniques of mediation and collaborative problem-solving is essential in today's business environment. By fostering open communication, active listening, and a solution-oriented mindset, we can build stronger relationships, enhance teamwork, and ultimately achieve greater success in our professional lives.

# Chapter 11: Developing Interpersonal Skills for Effective Communication

## Building Rapport and Trust

In the fast-paced and competitive business environment, effective collaboration and communication are key to achieving success. One of the most fundamental aspects of building strong relationships in the workplace is establishing rapport and trust. When employees are able to connect with one another and trust their colleagues, productivity and teamwork flourish. In this subchapter, we will explore the techniques for building rapport and trust that are essential for mastering business communication in the dynamic business environment.

First and foremost, active listening is a crucial skill that fosters rapport and trust. When engaging in conversations, employees must give their undivided attention to the speaker, maintain eye contact, and show genuine interest. By actively listening, employees demonstrate respect for their colleagues and create an atmosphere of trust and understanding.

Another powerful technique to build rapport is to find common ground. Employees can initiate conversations that go beyond work-related topics, such as hobbies, shared interests, or personal experiences. By discovering shared connections, individuals can establish a deeper bond and develop a sense of camaraderie within the team. This shared understanding helps to create an environment where employees feel comfortable expressing their ideas and opinions.

Transparency and honesty are also essential elements in building trust. Employees should always strive to maintain open and honest communication with their colleagues. This means being upfront about challenges, admitting mistakes, and providing constructive feedback. When employees feel that they can trust their colleagues to be transparent and honest, it fosters a culture of trust and encourages open dialogue.

Non-verbal communication plays a significant role in building rapport and trust as well. Simple gestures like maintaining a positive body language, offering a warm smile, and using appropriate facial expressions can go a long way in creating a comfortable and welcoming atmosphere. Employees should also be mindful of their tone of voice and ensure that it conveys respect and empathy.

Lastly, consistent follow-through is crucial for establishing trust. Employees should strive to meet deadlines, deliver on promises, and communicate effectively. By consistently following through on commitments, employees demonstrate their reliability and dedication, which in turn, builds trust among colleagues.

Building rapport and trust is a continuous process that requires effort and commitment. By actively practicing the techniques outlined in this subchapter, employees can create a supportive and collaborative work environment that drives success in the competitive business environment.

**Empathy and Emotional Intelligence**

Empathy and Emotional Intelligence in a Business Environment

In today's fast-paced and competitive business environment, it is essential for employees to possess not only technical skills but also strong interpersonal abilities. One of the most vital qualities that can greatly contribute to success in the workplace is empathy and emotional intelligence. In this subchapter, we will delve into the significance of these traits and explore ways to master them for effective collaboration in a business setting.

Empathy, often described as the ability to understand and share the feelings of others, plays a crucial role in building positive relationships with colleagues, clients, and stakeholders. By putting ourselves in others' shoes, we can better comprehend their perspectives, needs, and concerns. This enables us to respond with understanding, kindness, and support, thereby fostering a harmonious work environment. Empathy allows us to connect on a deeper level, build trust, and create meaningful collaborations that drive business success.

Emotional intelligence, on the other hand, refers to the capacity to recognize, understand, and manage our own emotions, as well as those of others. It involves being aware of our own emotions and how they influence our actions, as well as being attuned to the emotions of those around us. By developing emotional intelligence, we can navigate conflicts effectively, resolve problems efficiently, and inspire others to perform at their best. It allows us to adapt to changing circumstances, communicate with clarity and empathy, and make sound decisions even in high-pressure situations.

To cultivate empathy and emotional intelligence, it is crucial to actively listen to others, seeking to understand their experiences and perspectives without judgment. We should strive to communicate effectively, both verbally and nonverbally, displaying empathy through our words, tone, and body language. It is also essential to develop self-awareness by reflecting on our own emotions, triggers, and biases. By understanding ourselves better, we can regulate our emotions and respond to others in a more empathetic and compassionate manner.

In conclusion, empathy and emotional intelligence are indispensable skills in the modern business environment. By embracing these qualities, employees can foster stronger relationships, enhance collaboration, and boost overall productivity. Developing empathy and emotional intelligence enables us to connect with others on a deeper level, understand their needs, and respond with empathy and understanding. In today's competitive business landscape, mastering these skills is essential for effective communication, successful collaborations, and overall professional growth.

## Handling Difficult Conversations

In the dynamic and fast-paced business environment, employees often find themselves faced with difficult conversations that require a delicate touch. Whether it's addressing a performance issue, delivering bad news, or resolving conflicts, mastering the art of handling difficult conversations is essential for effective collaboration in the business world.

This subchapter aims to equip employees with valuable techniques and strategies to navigate challenging discussions, fostering a more positive and productive work environment. By incorporating these skills into their communication toolbox, employees can build stronger relationships, promote understanding, and achieve successful outcomes in difficult conversations.

The first step in handling difficult conversations is to approach them with a mindset of empathy and understanding. It is essential to listen actively and attentively to the other person's perspective, acknowledging their emotions and concerns. By creating a safe and non-judgmental space, employees can foster open and honest dialogue, leading to better problem-solving and mutual resolutions.

Next, effective communication techniques such as using "I" statements, staying calm, and maintaining a respectful tone are crucial. Employees should focus on expressing their thoughts and feelings without attacking or blaming the other person. This approach encourages a more constructive conversation and reduces defensiveness, allowing both parties to find common ground and work towards a solution.

Furthermore, mastering non-verbal communication is imperative in difficult conversations. Employees should be aware of their body language, maintaining eye contact, using appropriate gestures, and displaying active listening cues. Non-verbal cues can significantly impact the overall message and help create a more positive and empathetic atmosphere during challenging discussions.

Another essential aspect is practicing effective problem-solving and negotiation skills. Employees should be prepared to offer potential solutions, brainstorm ideas, and be open to compromise. By focusing on finding win-win situations, employees can foster collaboration and reach mutually beneficial agreements.

Lastly, it is vital to follow up on difficult conversations to ensure that the agreed-upon actions are implemented and any unresolved issues are addressed promptly. This demonstrates accountability and commitment to the resolution process, fostering trust and strengthening working relationships.

In conclusion, mastering the art of handling difficult conversations is an essential skill for employees in the business environment. By approaching these conversations with empathy, active listening, effective communication, and problem-solving techniques, employees can navigate challenging discussions successfully. Through these strategies, employees can foster a positive work environment, build stronger relationships, and achieve productive outcomes in difficult conversations.

## Networking and Relationship Building

Networking and Relationship Building in the Business Environment

In today's highly competitive business environment, networking and relationship building have become crucial skills for employees at all levels. The ability to establish and maintain meaningful connections with colleagues, clients, and industry peers can greatly enhance one's professional success and contribute to overall business growth. This subchapter explores the importance of networking and provides valuable techniques for effective relationship building in the business world.

Networking is more than simply exchanging business cards or attending industry events. It is about cultivating mutually beneficial relationships that can open doors to new opportunities, knowledge sharing, and support. Employees who actively engage in networking build a network of resources that can provide guidance, advice, and insights when needed. By nurturing these relationships, individuals can also gain access to new clients, partnerships, and career advancement possibilities.

To excel in networking, employees should adopt a strategic approach. This involves identifying key individuals or groups within their industry, attending relevant events, and actively participating in professional associations. By positioning themselves as active contributors, employees can establish credibility and gain visibility among their peers. Furthermore, leveraging social media platforms and online communities can expand networking opportunities beyond traditional boundaries.

Building strong relationships is equally important. Effective relationship building entails developing trust, empathy, and effective communication skills. Employees should seek to understand the needs and challenges of their colleagues, clients, and partners and offer genuine assistance whenever possible. By demonstrating reliability, integrity, and a willingness to collaborate, employees can foster a positive reputation and become go-to individuals within their network.

Additionally, maintaining a diverse network is crucial. Employees should engage with individuals from various industries, backgrounds, and expertise areas. This diversity brings fresh perspectives, fosters innovation, and increases the likelihood of serendipitous connections that can lead to breakthroughs and new business opportunities.

Networking and relationship building are ongoing processes that require time, effort, and a genuine interest in others. By continuously nurturing these connections, employees can build a robust network that provides long-term benefits for themselves and their organizations.

In conclusion, networking and relationship building are essential skills for employees in the business environment. The ability to establish and maintain meaningful connections can lead to new opportunities, knowledge sharing, and support. By adopting a strategic approach, employees can effectively network with industry peers and expand their professional reach. Building strong relationships based on trust, empathy, and effective communication skills is equally important. Maintaining a diverse network further enhances creativity and increases the likelihood of serendipitous connections. By investing time and effort into networking and relationship building, employees can enhance their professional success and contribute to the overall growth of their organizations.

# Chapter 12: The Future of Business Communication

**Evolving Communication Trends**

In today's fast-paced business environment, effective communication is essential for successful collaboration and organizational growth. As technology continues to advance, communication trends are constantly evolving, and employees must stay abreast of these changes to remain competitive.

One of the most significant communication trends in the business environment is the increasing reliance on digital platforms. With the rise of email, instant messaging, and video conferencing, employees can connect with colleagues and clients across the globe in a matter of seconds. This has revolutionized the way we communicate, enabling real-time collaboration and breaking down geographical barriers.

Another emerging trend is the growing popularity of remote work. With the advent of cloud-based tools and mobile devices, employees can now work from anywhere, reducing the need for traditional face-to-face communication. Virtual team meetings and project management software have become integral to modern business operations, enabling seamless collaboration regardless of physical location.

Social media platforms have also transformed the way businesses communicate. Companies are utilizing platforms such as LinkedIn, Twitter, and Facebook to connect with customers, promote products, and build brand awareness. Employees need to understand the power of social media and how to leverage it for effective communication and networking within the business environment.

Furthermore, the increasing use of artificial intelligence (AI) and chatbots has streamlined communication processes. AI-powered chatbots can handle routine customer inquiries, freeing up employees to focus on more complex tasks. This technology has the potential to enhance efficiency and productivity, but employees must learn how to effectively integrate AI into their communication strategies.

As communication trends continue to evolve, it is crucial for employees to adapt and embrace new technologies and tools. Mastering these trends can lead to improved collaboration, increased efficiency, and enhanced professional growth. Organizations that are quick to adopt and adapt to these changing trends will have a competitive edge in the business environment.

In conclusion, the world of business communication is constantly evolving, driven by advances in technology and changing workplace dynamics. Employees must stay informed about the latest communication trends to remain effective and productive in the business environment. By embracing digital platforms, remote work, social media, and AI, employees can enhance their collaboration skills and contribute to the success of their organizations.

## Embracing Technological Advancements

Embracing Technological Advancements in Today's Business Environment

In today's rapidly evolving business environment, it is imperative for employees to embrace technological advancements in order to stay competitive and thrive in their respective industries. The integration of technology has revolutionized the way we communicate, collaborate, and conduct business overall. Therefore, it is crucial for employees to adapt and master these advancements to enhance their effectiveness in the workplace.

One of the most significant technological advancements that has reshaped business communication is the advent of digital platforms and tools. From email and instant messaging to video conferencing and project management software, these digital tools have streamlined communication processes, enabling employees to connect and collaborate with colleagues and clients from anywhere in the world. Embracing these tools allows for efficient and effective communication, resulting in improved productivity and faster decision-making.

Moreover, the rise of social media and online networking platforms has transformed the way businesses connect with their target audiences. Employees who are well-versed in leveraging these platforms can facilitate valuable connections, build strong professional networks, and enhance their company's online presence. By embracing social media, employees can stay up-to-date with industry trends, engage with customers, and even contribute to thought leadership discussions, positioning themselves and their organizations as leaders in their respective fields.

Technological advancements have also revolutionized data management and analysis. With the advent of big data and analytics tools, employees can now make data-driven decisions, identify trends and patterns, and gain valuable insights into customer behavior. By embracing these advancements, employees can enhance their problem-solving skills, develop innovative strategies, and contribute to the growth and success of their organizations.

However, it is important to remember that embracing technological advancements is not merely about learning how to use specific tools or platforms. It also requires a mindset shift towards continuous learning and adaptability. Employees should be open to exploring new technologies, attending training programs, and seeking out opportunities to enhance their digital literacy skills. By doing so, they can stay ahead of the curve and remain valuable assets in an ever-evolving business environment.

In conclusion, embracing technological advancements is crucial for employees in today's business environment. By adapting to digital tools, leveraging social media, and embracing data analysis, employees can enhance their communication, collaboration, and problem-solving skills. By continuously learning and adapting to new technologies, employees can stay competitive, contribute to their organizations' success, and thrive in their respective industries.

## Adapting to Changing Communication Needs

In today's fast-paced business environment, effective communication is crucial for successful collaboration. As technology continues to evolve, so do our communication needs. To thrive in this dynamic landscape, employees must be adaptive and embrace new methods of communication. This subchapter will provide valuable insights and techniques for mastering business communication in an ever-changing environment.

One of the most significant changes in recent years is the rise of remote work and virtual teams. With employees scattered across different locations, it is essential to utilize digital communication tools effectively. Platforms like video conferencing, instant messaging, and project management software have become indispensable for maintaining seamless collaboration. Understanding how to navigate these tools and adapt to remote work dynamics is vital for employees to stay connected and productive.

Another aspect to consider is the increasing reliance on mobile communication. Smartphones have become an extension of our professional lives, allowing us to access information and connect with others instantly. Employees need to be adept at leveraging mobile technology to communicate effectively on the go. Mobile-friendly apps and responsive design have become essential for businesses to ensure seamless communication across devices.

Furthermore, the changing communication landscape calls for employees to embrace cultural diversity and inclusivity. In today's globalized business environment, teams often consist of individuals from different cultural backgrounds. Understanding cultural nuances and adapting communication styles accordingly is crucial to avoid misunderstandings and foster a harmonious work environment.

Adapting to changing communication needs also involves honing one's written communication skills. With the prevalence of email and digital messaging, employees must be proficient in crafting concise, clear, and professional messages. Additionally, understanding the importance of tone and context in written communication is vital, as misinterpretations can easily arise in the absence of non-verbal cues.

Finally, embracing continuous learning is essential for adapting to evolving communication needs. Staying updated with the latest communication tools, techniques, and trends ensures employees remain effective and efficient communicators. Investing in professional development opportunities like workshops, webinars, or online courses can aid in enhancing communication skills.

In conclusion, mastering business communication in the ever-changing business environment requires employees to be adaptable and open to new methods of communication. By embracing remote work dynamics, utilizing mobile technology, respecting cultural diversity, honing written communication, and investing in continuous learning, employees can navigate the evolving communication landscape with confidence and thrive in their professional roles.

## Continuous Improvement and Lifelong Learning in Business Communication

In today's rapidly evolving business environment, effective communication is paramount to success. Whether you are a seasoned professional or a newcomer to the business world, the ability to communicate clearly and efficiently is crucial. However, communication skills are not something that can be learned once and applied throughout your career. They require continuous improvement and lifelong learning.

Continuous improvement in business communication involves constantly striving to enhance your skills and adapt to new trends and technologies. This is particularly important in today's digital age, where communication channels and platforms are constantly evolving. By staying updated on the latest communication tools and techniques, you can ensure that your messages are conveyed effectively and resonate with your intended audience.

Lifelong learning, on the other hand, goes beyond simply keeping up with the latest trends. It involves a mindset of curiosity and a willingness to explore new ideas and perspectives. By embracing lifelong learning, you can expand your knowledge base and gain a deeper understanding of various aspects of business communication. This can include areas such as cross-cultural communication, nonverbal communication, and persuasive writing, among others.

Continuous improvement and lifelong learning in business communication can benefit employees in numerous ways. Firstly, it enhances their ability to convey their ideas and messages clearly, leading to improved collaboration and productivity within the organization. Effective communication also fosters stronger relationships with clients, customers, and colleagues, ultimately contributing to the overall success of the business.

Moreover, continuous improvement and lifelong learning in business communication help employees adapt to changes in the business environment. As technology continues to reshape the way we communicate, those who are proactive in learning new tools and techniques will be better equipped to navigate these changes. By embracing continuous improvement and lifelong learning, employees can future-proof their careers and remain relevant in an ever-evolving business landscape.

To foster continuous improvement and lifelong learning in business communication, organizations can provide training programs and resources that focus on enhancing communication skills. This can include workshops, seminars, online courses, and mentoring programs. Additionally, employees should be encouraged to seek out opportunities for self-improvement, such as attending industry conferences, joining professional associations, and participating in networking events.

In conclusion, continuous improvement and lifelong learning in business communication are crucial for employees operating in today's dynamic business environment. By continuously striving to enhance their communication skills and embracing a mindset of lifelong learning, employees can effectively adapt to changes, collaborate more efficiently, and contribute to the overall success of their organizations.

# Conclusion: Mastering Business Communication for Effective Collaboration

In today's fast-paced business environment, effective communication is crucial for successful collaboration. Whether you are an entry-level employee or a seasoned professional, mastering business communication techniques can significantly contribute to your success in the workplace. This subchapter aims to summarize the key takeaways from the book "Mastering Business Communication: Techniques for Effective Collaboration" and provide employees in the business environment with actionable insights to enhance their communication skills.

Throughout this book, we have explored various aspects of business communication, including verbal and non-verbal communication, written communication, active listening, and effective presentation skills. By understanding these techniques and applying them in your daily interactions, you can foster better relationships with colleagues, clients, and stakeholders, leading to improved collaboration and overall organizational success.

One of the fundamental lessons emphasized in this book is the importance of clear and concise communication. In a business environment where time is of the essence, being able to convey your message effectively and efficiently is crucial. By using simple and straightforward language, avoiding jargon, and structuring your communication in a logical manner, you can ensure that your ideas are understood by others.

Active listening is another crucial component of effective business communication. By actively engaging in conversations, paying attention to both verbal and non-verbal cues, and asking clarifying questions, you can demonstrate your interest and understanding, fostering stronger connections with your colleagues and enhancing collaboration.

Written communication skills are also vital in today's business world, where emails, reports, and memos are the primary means of conveying information. By mastering the art of writing clear, concise, and professional messages, you can ensure that your ideas are accurately communicated, avoiding misunderstandings and potential conflicts.

Furthermore, this book has provided practical tips for delivering impactful presentations. By structuring your presentations effectively, using visual aids, and utilizing storytelling techniques, you can capture your audience's attention, convey your message persuasively, and inspire action.

In conclusion, mastering business communication techniques is essential for effective collaboration in the business environment. By applying the lessons learned in this book, employees can enhance their communication skills, build stronger relationships, and contribute to the overall success of their organizations. Remember, effective communication is a continuous learning process, so never stop refining and improving your skills to become a master communicator in the dynamic world of business.

Milton Keynes UK
Ingram Content Group UK Ltd.
UKHW020942221123
433051UK00020B/1003